# You can't make this $h#t Up!

How to Avoid Having SEX When He's in The Mood and You're Not

by

Sandy von Ellm

DORRANCE
PUBLISHING CO
EST. 1920
PITTSBURGH, PENNSYLVANIA 15238

Dorrance Publishing Co
585 Alpha Drive
Pittsburgh, PA 15238
Visit our website at *www.dorrancebookstore.com*

ISBN: 978-1-6470-2170-2
eISBN: 978-1-6470-2997-5

# Dedication

———————— ⠿ ————————

To my Mom, it's impossible to thank you for everything you've done, from loving me unconditionally and teaching me to embrace life. Thank you so much for spending your life loving me and taking such good care of all my needs. I'm so proud to call you Mom and even happier to call you my best friend.

To my husband, Michael—it's a privilege to share my dreams, my life, and my love with you.

To my children, Maria and Liam—your growth provides a constant source of joy and pride. You taught me to be free and to follow my dreams.

To all my friends who provided their input, your stories delivered lots of laughter and tears. Friends make the world a little lighter, a little brighter, and a whole lot more fun!

To all my the readers, I hope that you have at least half as much fun in the reading of this book as I've had in the writing.

# Introduction

I wrote this book for all the women who share similar experiences. It was a thought that developed over time after having conversations with so many friends and realizing that we all share a common bond. We often joked about the excuses that we gave to our husbands, lovers, or boyfriends, but came to the conclusion that no matter how long we've been in a relationship, at some point we have all had to come up with an excuse to avoid doing "It."

Most of us experience healthy, loving relationships, but because of work schedules, kids, and responsibilities, we are not always in the mood to do "It." Contrary to popular belief, honesty is not always the best policy, as we do not want to hurt our partners' feelings. As a result, we create "Excuses." My friends and I have often laughed ourselves to tears while sharing unique excuses we've given our husbands or partners.

We have all heard the classic excuse of "Honey, I have a headache." We have definitely evolved our repertoire since utilizing this oldie but goodie. My personal go-to has always been "Sorry, I can't tonight because I have my period." However, if this excuse doesn't work for you, feel free to choose one of the many funny options provided in this book.

# Grooming

I smell down there. I need a bath.

Haven't shaved my legs.

It's as thick as a forest down there!

I haven't brushed my teeth yet.

I need to bathe (stay in the tub/shower until he falls asleep)

I have bad breath.

I can't; I just put cream on my face.

# Bodily Functions

I feel bloated!

I am too tired!

I feel sick.

I think I have a yeast infection.

I have an upset stomach!

# Medical Conditions

I have a cold.

I have a rash.

I am too depressed.

I am having hot flashes.

My back hurts.

I am getting a cold sore.

My hemorrhoids are flaring.

I forgot to take "the pill".

Are you serious, I am pregnant!

# Body Aches

I am cramping.

Arthritis is flaring up again.

I just worked out and I am sore.

My nipples are sensitive.

# No Time or Energy

There is too much on my mind. I am way too stressed!

I need my sleep; I have an early morning meeting.

I am too tired from cooking and cleaning.

It's late!

# His Issues

No, because you only last a few seconds.

No, because the Viagra lasts too long.

You Smell. You need to shower.
(pretend you fell asleep by the time he comes back)

What do you mean? It's not your birthday.

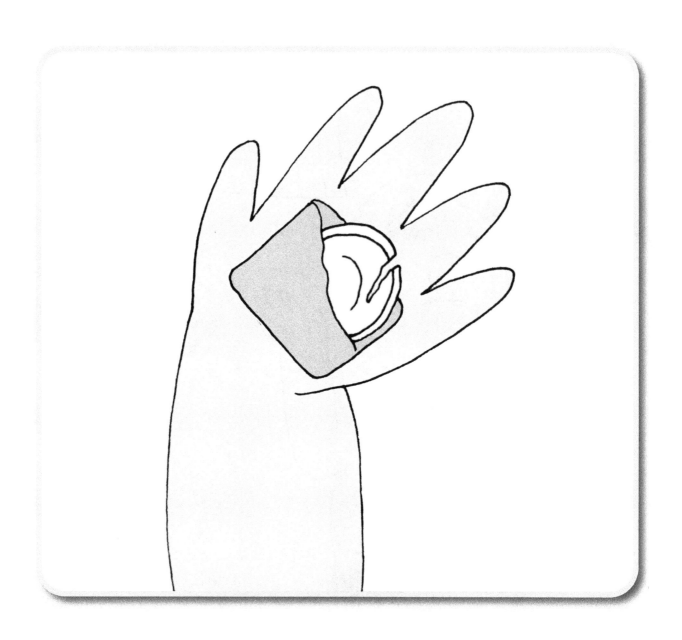

We have a bad batch of condoms.

# Other Distractions

I can't. The dogs are in the room watching us.

Seriously? Your parents are sleeping in the room next door.

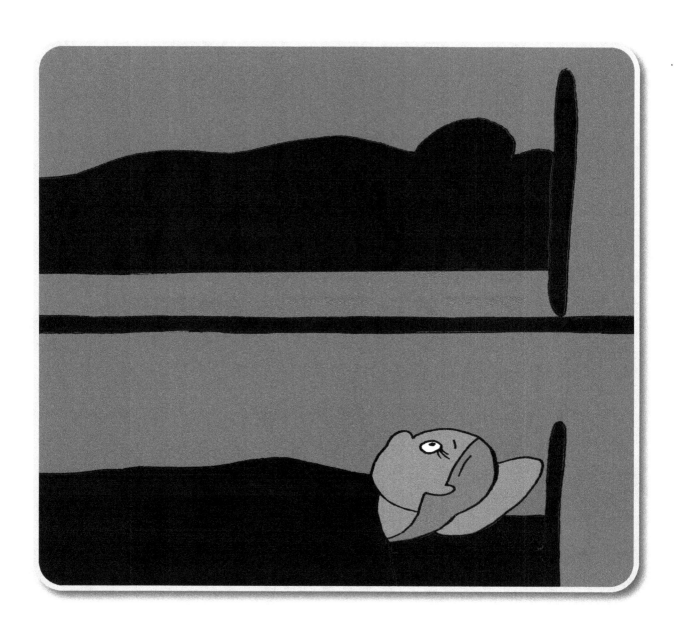

I can't do" it" in someone else's home
(they may hear us or we may stain the sheets).

It's not our scheduled day to do "it".

You're too noisy. We will wake up the kids.

I am too upset with:

_____ Kids,

_____ Work,

_____ Family,

_____ All the Above.

Are you !#!!.(Start an argument to avoid sex.)

Not tonight, I have a headache.

CPSIA information can be obtained
at www.ICGtesting.com
Printed in the USA
JSHW021445261121
20719JS00003B/82